About the Author

Marion Berndt was born in 1968 in Northern Germany. She is a primary school teacher out of conviction and a writer out of passion. At the age of five she had already announced to her family she would be a teacher and "book writer". She has been teaching since 1994. After studying "writing" at the Axel-Andersson-Akademie in Hamburg, in 2014 she started publishing school material in Germany. In fact, she loves writing in different genres. "Lockdown-Poetry" is her first poetry collection which she started writing during the worldwide covid lockdown in 2020.

Lockdown-Poetry

Marion Berndt

Lockdown-Poetry

Olympia Publishers
London

www.olympiapublishers.com
OLYMPIA PAPERBACK EDITION

Copyright © Marion Berndt 2022

The right of Marion Berndt to be identified as author of
this work has been asserted in accordance with sections 77 and 78
of the Copyright, Designs and Patents Act 1988.

All Rights Reserved

No reproduction, copy or transmission of this publication
may be made without written permission.
No paragraph of this publication may be reproduced,
copied or transmitted save with the written permission of the
publisher, or in accordance with the provisions
of the Copyright Act 1956 (as amended).

Any person who commits any unauthorised act in relation to
this publication may be liable to criminal
prosecution and civil claims for damage.

A CIP catalogue record for this title is
available from the British Library.

ISBN: 978-1-80074-461-5

This is a work of fiction.
Names, characters, places and incidents originate from the writer's
imagination. Any resemblance to actual persons, living or dead, is
purely coincidental.

First Published in 2022

Olympia Publishers
Tallis House
2 Tallis Street
London
EC4Y 0AB

Printed in Great Britain

Dedication

#amwriting my #poetry into your heart
for eternity…

For Richard

Acknowledgments

Thank you to my family and friends for always encouraging me to follow my love and my dreams. Thanks to Christel, Tanja, Carrie and Taize from DeadLetterRadioPodcast for strengthening my self-confidence and pushing me to try and submit my manuscript and to all the great people at Olympia Publishers for your kindness and trust in my poetry. Last not least at all: Thank you, Richard. Without you nothing would have happened at all. You know what I mean. x

Lockdown-Poetry

And suddenly
both our worlds stood still.
For the first time.
At the same time.

We had read
our silence for years.
Now time to talk and listen.
For the first time.
At the same time.
Coincidence?

The blind years...

"I've seen a miracle.
I've seen you…"

"Me too!"

Gloomy London street.
It is approaching midnight.
Hottest summer date…

One night
he was suddenly standing there.
He didn't say a word
I could hear.
He just stood and stared
on his lips a mysterious smile.
But then we talked
with our eyes…

One day someone falls into your life
and you are unable
to remember how you survived
the day before…

Only one time in one lifetime two lives
give each other a smile
promising a future…

It's in your smile

*When I think of you,
and I do all the way,
I think about
how to get through the day.*

*And when I think of you
— see your face in front of me,
know what you would say,
feel you close to me.*

*But all your words so honestly and touch so true,
could not let me survive, because it's all in your smile!*

*I could feel, see and hear, all the world gives.
All this would be nothing without your smile!*

*Everything my heart hopes.
That's all in your smile
and it changed my life…*

<u>Often</u>

Often I wondered what was on your mind
when we first met. You so undecided.
Endless seconds in one look.
My encouraging smile.
What was on your tongue
before you started to run?

All my love buried
deep in my heart.
For so long hurt,
numb and sore,
sleepwalker
till there was
you…

Light is easy to love.
Show me your darkness.
I'm not scared of that place.
I used to live there myself…

<u>Wings</u>

I worked hard to grow my wings,
yet you had to come to prove to me
I can fly.
This love is the wind.
Fly with me!
High!

Come into your heart.
It's a heavenly place.
I'm here to guard your light.
So you can find the way…

Do you love him?
Then fight his fears.
If you do love him,
you'll fight his darkness.
You love him, don't you?
Then fight for him
without fighting…

*I love… I don't know
if I'm doing it well,
but I do my best to make it right…*

Sunday morning

A through and through positive emptiness.
No crowds in our heads. Everything is just feeling.
At home. Quiet.
Inner peace.
My hands with yours in the game.
Silent joy.
Lost in your eyes, mirror of my soul.
Satisfaction in our smile.
Humor in the crumbs in your beard.
All masks stored.
Tucked away just behind the rising steam
from the coffee mugs.
Safety.
Alone. Together.
Love. Warmth. Devotion.
Unconditionally.
Our day.
Happiness, perfection, fulfillment.
Just be. Me here.
You
at the other end of the world.

<u>Small world</u>

I come
from a small world.
Please, can you help me to grow?
And if there's a small world inside you,
may I nourish
this sacred place in you?

I wonder
what would happen
if I lit a candle in your heart?
Could it make you see
what you've never seen?
Would it make you feel safe and warm?
Would you just know
I could never do you any harm?

All my life

Trying to escape from what I want
to hold tight forever.
Pushing away
what I've been longing for all my life…

Help me find the answer,
I do not dare.
He's longing for her vibes.
He's waiting for her words.
He's following each of her moves.
He's pretending he doesn't care.
What is it they share?

Calm… ssshhh!
I am just nudging your world a little
so that your heart doesn't stand still…

Why?

Why do I love you, you ask me?
Why do I love you?
Well, I do.

I never found a thousand words for it.
As soon as there was one, it had disappeared again.

Why do I love you?
I don't know.
Why do I love you?
I cannot help it.

I accept it. I live with it.
I grow into this love step by step.

Why do I love you?
You know what?
Find out for yourself!
Because only what you feel,
you probably believe!

What if?

What if it's not about adventure
but about depth?
What if it's not about giving up
but about durability?
What if it's not about loss again
but about growth?
What if it's not about the happy ending
but the story?
What if...
I gave it a try?

Sometimes I need someone not that close
— yet even closer...

Since you're there

Since you've sneaked into my life,
I stand up in the morning with a smile.
My day a collection of thoughts of love and light.
My actions supported by good energy.
Your blessing is in everything I see.
You bring out the best in me!

I see your forefinger. You slow me in my haste.
I hear your humor.
With me my burden you share.
You make me realize. You give me a reason.
I follow my destiny since you're there.

Humble, to go side by side.
Even if I can feel your sorrow,
since you're there, I trust the way.
I know you share your way with me.
You are the voice of my reason,
which holds in check my cheeky heart.
Your soul is the most precious gift in the world!

Since you've sneaked into my life,
I go to bed in the evening with a grateful smile.
Just knowing that you're there.
Just knowing that you exist somewhere.

Secret room

We live together
in a secret room inside
— just you and me —
our place to hide.
The room keeping safe
the dreams we share.
Just meet me there…
Good night!

**And suddenly
our worlds stood still...**

"I know you are there...
If you should need support in any way
... I'm here."

*"If anyone is feeling
a bit scared at the moment
... I'm here."*

How long is now?

Too long…
an eternity…
How long is now?
Our lives…
braked.

How long is now?

Too long…
an eternity…
How long is now?
Our reunion…
deferred again.

<u>Hallo</u>

This is just a quick "hallo" to my friend.
Hope to see you soon again!
Just wanted to tell you, that I miss you.
Just wanted to tell you, I am still true.

If I cannot be more than your friend,
let me be that until the very end.
Must let you know that I will not drop you.
Must let you know that I am there for you.

I could not stand
to be "nothing" for you,
for you are "everything" to me.

Words… cannot be said often enough
when they are true.
Words… cannot be heard often enough
when they make you smile.

I'm here

Just one heart needs to open.
One word will break the ice.
One touch can kill the darkness.
Union will make it light.

One little conversation can light dark thoughts,
heavy loads, hard times.
One little conversation can open new perspectives.
One little conversation
can change two lives...

Open your eyes.
Maybe there is already someone
walking with you...

I cannot take it from you.
I cannot make it for you.
I can only feel you
and sail by your side...

When time goes by

When time goes by and all things change,
when no one stays, nothing remains,
when darkness falls and dangers rule,
when there is pain and solitude
then I'm here and there are you…

When you make a fist I open it
and put my hand into yours…

This is a quiet time — not peaceful.
An uncertain time — yet not dark.
We make a difference
to each other…

Let me make you smile.
Let me touch your heart.
Let me fill your soul.
Allow yourself to give up control…

*You know
I don't believe
that it is so simple.
You know I doubt
love could ever be so easy.
You know my heart whispers:
"You must give it a try…"*

Let me be your refuge
and your shelter.
Let me be your solace
and if you want to
be my storyteller…

There's a little voice

There's a little voice,
a continual supplication.
She will never be demanding, outrageous
and yet she will never vanish.

She is a slight whisper,
a silent wind.
She's a balmy breeze, unobtrusive
will be seething deep within.

She's my secret path finder,
forces me to see.
She is my guide, completely penetrant
and I'll never escape.

She's my secret dream,
loves me sight unseen.
She's my most faithful friend, unconditionally,
will go with me to the very end...

Moon and Sun

How much brighter was the Moon,
if he'd not flee from the Sun.
Moon and Sun united,
two Suns in the universe as one.

Look, look at me.
Follow my track
and shine through my light.
Let me be your Sun.

We go the same way to the same aim,
serve the big whole
as Sun and Moon
in the interplay.

When darkness goes,
we meet at the threshold
and you alone decide
if you leave your orbit,
if Moon and Sun unite.

As

As the Sun must trust the Moon
to follow her home,
The Moon must believe
in the everglow of the Sun
to warm him
forever…

My truth

Torn between two worlds,
yet only one world is true.
Wherever I go I see your smile.
Present in my heart whatever I do.

Each instant sensing you.
Scared to lose myself
without and inside you.

I know
we take the long way home,
always doing the best we can do.
Loving the way only we can love,
don't leave me alone, my truth…

<u>Chances</u>

Accepting the chances hard times offer.
Using opportunities to grow together.
Taking courage to finally try.
Living in the now.
No more "What if?" or "Why?"
Simply falling into the gift to walk through all this
side by side…

Let's dream about the stars.
Let's dream about the moon.
Maybe our wish is the same,
then we can make it come true…
Good night!

Reading the silence...

*"Read my heart
for it is beating
inside yours..."*

Can you read my world behind?
Can you vibrate in my language?
Only you can hear the voice
of my heart…

Though I'm living
deep inside you,
sense into each corner
of your soul,
you are my beautiful mystery…

My love is always with you
a warming glimmer in your heart.

**Heart web**

Do you see me now?
Yes… your image, your smile, your eyes,
your look…

Do you hear me now?
Yes… your voice, your peace, your determination,
your song…

Do you smell me now?
Yes… your presence, your care, your strength,
your balance…

Do you taste me now?
Yes… your fear, your grief, your weakness,
your anger…

Do you feel me now?
Yes… your heart…

*You remind me of
what butterflies feel like…*

                              I can feel
                         you are here with me.
                              Melting away.
                          Your heart stealing
                           this little moment
                                of bliss
                               with me…

Wonderful to feel
the waves
of your heart spilling over…
to mine!

Heart in heart

Heart in heart means
never feeling loneliness
even at the end of the world.

Heart in heart means
feeling love, warmth
even if the other is far away.

Heart in heart means
always feeling safe
even if you love in separation.

Heart in heart will
only be achieved in one way:
When the heart beats the reason!

The door

Opening the door
between two hearts
against all fear,
against all doubt.
Entering with astonished eyes
into the other soul's landscape.
Wandering carefully
into the magic forest
of familiar and challenge
hand in hand…

Knock, knock!

Woke up this morning,
someone kept knocking
on my heart's door
very insistently.
Now my innermost
is so warm.
Could it be
the one came in?

Breaking dawn.
Tears in my throat.
All your warmth is in my heart.
You must be cold.
Here inside me
your heart
has a life of its own…

Silent ways

I closed my eyes and spoke to you
in a thousand silent ways.
That's why I always know for sure
what your lasting silence says…

Hunch of an instant
when the silence is shouting,
the nothing says all.

Swimming.
Diving. Sinking.
Holding my breath. Washed away.
Liquid. Emotional wave.
Drowning in words swallowed.
Nearly choking.
Shall I dare?
Flood of words I crave to say.
Transformed
into tears again…

Do you know someone
who's almost bursting to talk, to share?
But he was taught to always be strong
and fight through life alone.
One day he'll feel
he is safe
to open his heart.
It's not the time to walk alone
— not any more…

I'm scared
to lose my dream,
that dreaming might be
better than having.
Is finding out always better
than regretting?

You

You make me smile.
You let me implode.
You dry my tears.
You let them flow.
You are my despair
and at the same time my hope.
You give me confidence and strength
and thus rob.
Over my darkest shadows you lift me.
Panic butterflies in the belly.

You do all this with me,
you do it to me,
you give it to me.
You tear the floor
on which I stand securely.
You are the path I go.

In my life, you are all that is.
That is why I am you.

__If__

If.
If you are in need.
If you are in need of someone
just one
to join you in your silence,
let me be someone…
Just if…

*Our night talks
are the deepest…*

___Sometimes___

*Sometimes
you don't need words.
Sometimes you just need
the presence that says:
"Always."*

Silence is carrying
the loving thoughts
and feelings of the one
who loves you…

When words are speechless.
When rhymes fail.
When text is empty,
our hearts prevail…

I sense you are swimming
whipped back and forth
by your deep dark emotional sea.
But much more grueling
than the tide inside you
is the fact that it makes you
an open book
to me…

You read my darkest chapters.
I roam in your deepest valleys.
We both know who will stay...

There are a thousand ways
to love a silent angel...

Some things cannot be expressed
by words...not even in poetry.

Just imagine
I'm lying next to you right now... calm.
You needn't say a word.
I just sense.
Just try to feel
I'm putting my arms around you right now... warm.
You can just let go.
I just touch... your soul.

And when I turn around tonight,
I feel you are there...

And then

And then
there is this deep warmth in my chest
and I know you are with me.
And then
there is this silent flow in my heart
and I know you let yourself fall
into my love…

I love the night.
Darkness creeping into my eyes
making me see
my dream lying next to me.
Silence echoing in my ears
like a caress of her voice
so near…

That's when

When his inner moves shake you
as soon as you are near.
When you sense his heat rising
as soon as your message appears.
When the loving flow between two hearts
makes you smile
while gliding into sleep.
Then you know…

With yours

And when you can't sleep tonight,
I'll stay awake with you.
And when you terribly freeze inside,
I'll shiver, too.
And when your fears burst out as heat,
let me try to cool.
And when you cry yourself to sleep,
feel my heartbeat in synch with yours…
Sleep peacefully!

Dialogue

"Talk to me
the way
only you and me can talk —
or any other…"

I know times are hard.
I feel you at your limits.
I sense your hope falling apart.
But someone's relying on you,
fighting with you
each and every minute…

No matter

No matter how long.
No matter how far.
No matter how difficult.
No matter how hard.
No matter what…

So close

*So close,
she is so close to you.
You make her so sad.
Worst enemy to yourself
— so hard.*

*So close,
she is so close to you.
Bring her to silence,
suppress your light
— so clear.*

*So close,
she is so close to you.
You deserve her.
Fear of this love…
— so true.*

If you are as happy as you claim to be
then why do you stay close to me?

Hunch

I have a hunch…
that you've found
what you need
right here.
And I have a hunch…
that you take it
whenever
you are in need.
I have a hunch
you are with me…

*Like ice-cold drops
dripping from an ice cube,
running down my spine.
Like boiling hot mist
that caresses my heart…
when you think of me.*

If I just dared

*If I just dared,
my life would finally turn around
and I wouldn't be scared
any more.
If I dared,
what would it be like?
Would it work?
Of the "What if" I'm scared.
If I just dared,
I'd miss so many rides
on the merry-go-round...*

A voice I love to bath in.
Two blue eyes to get lost in.
A smile that ignites mine.
A soul I can drown in.
A heart so confused...
so sad... so blind...

Refugee

I'm not just a vagabond, I'm on the run.
You see through me. I run away.
I run like the wind day and night.
I know I belong to you,
but I do not feel it.
I want to be with you,
but a power pulls me away.
There is no reason to flee.
Tell me why I do!
I'm not just a vagabond, I'm on the run.

You remind me of all I missed.
Illusion of harmony, which does not remain.
My past's curse… Please believe me, it's not you.
It's me. Condemned to be alone.

If you let me down, I would understand.
Thank you for being there and walking by my side.
No matter how far I run, thanks to you, I know:
To return it's never too late.

You're so vulnerable.
I'm scared to scare you,
afraid to crack you.
Would you break?
Would you crumble,
if I wrapped you
in my light?

*Can you imagine how much energy is imprisoned
in unfulfilled longings? Can you?*

When I feel weak I talk to you
even without you here.
Maybe it helps when you talk to me.
Despite the distance be sure I'll hear…

I was strongest in my weakest hours,
but I know I couldn't be in your presence…

Your smile
speaks another language
than your eyes…
Your words
have another color
than your heart…

Empty

Empty eyes
behind a forced smile.
Empty heart
echoing tears of a forced soul.
Empty years
went by…

So tired

I'm so tired.
You suck me.
I'm exhausted.
You're denying
that you're sucking.

I am where you are.
You are not here.
I'm close to you.
Only from yourself you flee.

I'm so sad.
You are pretending.
I'm so tired.
You're not lending
yourself an ear.

I'm so tired…
… so tired…

Never

Hardly awake
freezing to my inner core.
Tears wash me.
Never felt closer.
Never lived deeper inside you before.
Existing in two skins.
Sadness,
side by side we walk through.
Never lonesome, never homeless,
never less apart from you.

A certain someone
in a certain place
should be asleep.
What thoughts are running?
What feelings go so deep?
Or maybe
— just a little maybe…
It's a little bit me?

__It happened this morning__

This morning
I gently caressed your heart.
Did you sense it?
Your cheeks in my palms
as a hunch on your skin.
My finger wandering over your forehead
with all tenderness I have.
My smile flooding your sleeping face.
Did you sense my loving presence?
When you took that deep breath,
did you inhale all my love?
Did your eyes open when my soul whispered,
"Good morning! Get up!"

Your soul clings to mine.
Can you feel the pull?

Bad night

*After a bad night
bruised in the morning,
bouncing up and down,
more and more exhausted.
Struggling all day
longing for deliverance.
Longing for a hideaway
my soul knows…*

I'll always fight for you, strengthen your love for life,
always dye your point of view in all colors so bright.
I'll always encourage your spirit of discovery
and dive into your childlike passion with you.
I'll always support finding ways to help you make
your sweetest dreams come true.
I'll never get tired of loving you
so that your self-love may endlessly grow.
I'll never stop fighting for you…

<u>Carry</u>

When shadows run around in your brain,
your forehead settles in deep wrinkles,
the lump continues to grow in your throat,
only feelings you repress again.
Then think of me: I'll carry you.
I love you.

If your world immersed in dusk,
your heart is deprived of any joy.
Firm belief is a foreign word for you,
clarity blurred of whirling spray.
Then think of me: I'll carry you.
I love you.

If your own voice fails you,
thoughts no longer come to light.
If confusion displaced by despair,
your mind keeps your soul tied.
Then think of me: I'll carry you.
I love you.

Call for you

*Often I sit in darkness
and call for you.
Often I sit in sunshine
and long for you.
Often I sit in the cold
and feel warmth in you.
Often I know it must be this way
and you feel it deep inside, too.*

Winter may be long,
but I'll walk with you
through the snow…

Hidden

I am grateful
that you allow yourself
to accept what I can give
in your quiet shy way.
I always sense
your hesitating heart
being warmed
by my modest means
to make you poetry.
And I know
you know
that I know
and that's our bravery.
Hidden.
But not hiding away…

Here with me...

Even in the worst of times
for a short while
my life is perfect
when I read your voice.
And the darkest place
in my head shines
when I see
you are here with me
my heart wants no choice…

I don't claim to be perfect.
I surely annoy you, tease you,
trigger something,
say stupid things.
I'm emotional, impulsive.
But you'll never find anyone anywhere
who cares more, loves more…
and more…each day.

So sudden, so deep

Sometimes.
So sudden.
So deep.
Grateful soul.
Smiling happiness.
Music
on the chords
of my heart.
Feeling
a tenderness
so warm for you
— just you…

The bridge

We've never been closer
than we are now.
We built a solid bridge
from shore to shore.
None of a thousand miles
could keep us apart.
When you feel like it
knock at the door of my heart…

There's someone.
There's always someone
who accompanies me through my day.
There's something.
There's always something
that makes my heart overflow.
And I'd never want it any other way…

Dark side of eternity

What a strange day!
I wander from room to room
knowing you're not here
yet searching for you.
My loneliness grows to emptiness
not feeling you by my side.
My energy fading without yours my life
— an infinite fight.

What an endless day!
My home feels like a tiny wardrobe.
I can hardly breathe.
How big my world is
when I see through your eyes.
How lost my heart is
when yours is not with mine.

What a never-ending hope so weak!
Will you at least be here
when we go to sleep?

Already waiting?
Waiting is our destiny…
Good reason to wait!

With and without you

Without you all is nothing.
With you nothing counts any more.
Love, formerly mostly only vain,
flows around and floods me today
like the wide sea.

Everything is possible with you.
Without you nothing goes.
Safety, in the past only fleetingly,
nourishes me and stands firm in me today,
is my love's bridge.

With you everything is alive in me.
Without you I give up.
Belief used to be no part of me,
fills my smallest space today
just knowing my truth…

Life is a dark room
lit by a single candle.
Don't leave me alone!

Maybe...

Maybe it's just okay now
to admit to be at the limit
and acknowledge
that that too
is okay...

                                                        Remember
there's always a way.
And when facing a dead end
it's all about jumping
from dream to reality...

Why does it have to be worse than bad
before man dares to change?
Why do you have to be on the floor
before you come back to stay?
Why?

Inner fight.
Totally exhausted.
That tug of war.
Longing — denying…
Fear but love.
Must give up my resistance!
Clear my mind.
I can own true love.
She is mine…

I really tried

I tried to push and pull you out of my heart,
but I wasn't strong enough.
I tried to wash you out,
but I almost drowned.
I wanted to kick you out,
but just hurt myself.
And then I tried to blow you out,
I only ran out of breath.
So I gave up fighting and let go
accepting my heart's your lifetime home…

One joy can drive out
a hundred worries.
Could it be I'm that joy for you?
Now I'm here, then I'm gone.
Each joy is just a short moment.
Spending your time waiting
for another and another one.
Only you can decide
to make our moment
never-ending…

Wanderer through time

*A wanderer through time
but not through space.
For ages my soul circles
the clam of your being.
Trapped in the orbit
of your heart…*

Fulfillment

Fight	Peace
Torn	Silence
Restlessness	Safety
Cold	Warmth
Futile Search	Recognition
Solitude	Togetherness
Fear	Courage
Unsecure future	Arrival
Resignation … Home!	

Stay close

*You find the right vibes
to hug my soul.
Stay close…
Your magnetic breath
pulls me back to you.
Stay close…
I'm addicted to your
idealistic dreams.
Stay close…
Your rose-colored glasses
see the best in me.
Stay close…
And your hypnotizing heartbeat
is why this life I chose.
I beg you:
Stay close…*

My angel

I feel weak,
you stand behind me.

I fear the headwinds,
you stand in front of me.

My life goes high and low,
you stand by my side.

Does my soul repose,
you are in the heart of mine.

Written in my soul
there is your name — for all time.

Maybe you just need someone in your life
who believes more in true love
— more than you doubt…

Fairy tales
&
happy endings…

"My life is a poem
written at a time
when I didn't know yet for whom…"

Poetry is...

Poetry is a butterfly
gently touching.
Poetry is a dove
always finding the one.
Poetry is a lion
silently roaring.
Poetry is a heart
second to none.
Poetry is you…

Countless times in my life
I longed for a hero,
begged for a miracle,
prayed for a fairy tale.
So many times.
Then you came
and I could see
I was supposed
to become a bestselling story
that just needed a plot twist…

Let me be your next chapter.
I'd never betray the author...

        If I painted my life, it would be
              a portrait of you...

                      All my life I was waiting for you.
                            I knew we had a date...

All my life
you were there.
You had no face,
but your energetic fingerprints
were all over my soul...

LOVE IS...

LOVE is…
the most powerful energy in life.

With love in your HEART…
you go every way,
you win every fight,
you enlighten every darkness,
you reach your aim.

The one who FOLLOWS his love,
never dreams in vain…

*You have a love
expressed in timeless words of beauty
in all possible honest actions…*

A hiding place.
A refuge
where there is peace.
A peace,
a special peace.
A home,
any place
where there is
you…

> There are many places in this world
> that I haven't seen.
> So many places I plan to visit.
> But there is only one place
> I crave to be…

Roads

You and me
know where we belong,
and just like
all roads lead to Rome,
each of our paths
will always
lead us back to
our home…

Home

*Your nearness
a romantic fireplace.
Your presence
delicious scent of a feast.
Your face smiling
cozy candlelight.
Your eyes
my window to the world.
Your voice
familiar wallpaper of my heart.
Your touch
pillow of peace.
Your soul
my home…*

Feeling so calm deep inside.
A silent joy in my heart
and I don't know why.
No, that's a lie!

<u>Lost</u>

*My heart has never been less lost
than since I've lost it.
I always know where it is.
Years ago it fell
into the right place.*

There's one decision
I'd make without thinking.
There's one choice
I'd never doubt…

My world is so little
for you are my world.
Yet, it is all universes in one…

*That one person
in the whole universe…*

Your presence
is my favorite song
forever humming
in the back
of my mind,
resonating
in the back
of my heart,
vibrating
in my root…

It feels
as if
there's
never been
a time
when I
didn't love you…

...the one you love

To rely on
the one you love...
Love yourself first.
Feel safe inside yourself.
Go the way to a "we".

To rely on
the one you love...
Rely on me.
If you need me,
I'll be there.
If you need yourself,
I'll stay away.
I trust you
that you never let go of yourself
— and me...

When it hurts to look back
and you are scared to look ahead,
look beside you and I'll be there...

That's me.
I'm yours
yet I alone own myself.
I dig deep
but from the mountain top.
I cross borders
but firmly set my limits.
I'll go far
but if you want me to
forever I'll stay…

That's you.
You are every paradox possible.
My soul not mine.
Mysterious open book.
Deepest high.
Close at any distance…

You keep my feet on the ground.
I'll keep your feet in the clouds.
That's how dream teams grow…

If he skids,
he looks for her hand.
If she sways,
he prevents her from falling…

I put my heart into your hand
knowing that I've done well…

My heart was always heavy and full.
But only when I knew I needed to make room in it for you,
did I find my own place there, too…

Look out of your window.
There's always a little blue
in the dark skies
and it's yours…

You are my star that lights up
with every heartbeat
guiding my path…

Each morning

*All of me
I find in you.
All of you resonates in me.
Each morning when I awake
I can't believe
we are true…*

The first
and the last.
Each day.
In all possible ways.
Thought.
Smile.
Heartbeat.
Breath.
The first
and the last.

A day like no other.
A day to remember.
Every day with you…

                              All is on the way.
                                   You and me,
                                     we are safe.
                          Today you cannot see,
                               what tomorrow
                                    will reveal…

              Where do we go?
       I don't know. But if you go I go.

              Where do we stay?
     Wherever you stay we stay together…

Lovers stay a little longer…

Sinking

When you go to sleep
I enjoy your growing surrender.
And when you go to sleep
your inner tension fading inside me.
When you go to sleep
we let go together.
And when you go to sleep
I sense your loving thought
because you smile knowing I'm here.

When you fall asleep
your hand tenderly sinks into mine.
And when you fall asleep
your voice in my head grows silent.
And when I fall asleep
we both fall into heavenly peace
looking forward to
a new daybreak together…

#amwriting my #poetry
into your heart for eternity… tbc.

www.ingramcontent.com/pod-product-compliance
Lightning Source LLC
LaVergne TN
LVHW041537060526
838200LV00037B/1023